11/18/93   For Sue: A best friend always
and one of mother's favorites!

Susie Kennedy

ONCE UPON A FAMILY

Once Upon A Family

Elizabeth Kennedy

Fithian Press
Santa Barbara, California

LIBRARY OF CONGRESS CATALOGING-IN-PUBLICATION DATA

Kenndey, Elizabeth Earhart, 1090-
    Once upon a family / Elizabeth Earhart Kennedy
        p.   cm.
    ISBN 0-931832-56-X
    1. Kennedy, Elizabeth Earhart, 1090-   --Childhood and youth.
    2. Detroit (Mich.)--Biography.   3. Ann Arbor (Mich.)--Biography.
    I. Title
    F574.D453K465   1990
    977.4'3404'092--dc20   90-33505
    [B]   CIP

Published by
FITHIAN PRESS
Post Office Box 1525
Santa Barbara, California, 93102

TABLE OF CONTENTS

PART I

1900 - 1910

EARLY YEARS

ONE DAY WHEN I was quite small, we were sitting around
the breakfast table, all six of us, literally a family circle, for
our big oak table was a round one. Breakfast was a full
course meal for which we children were expected to be on
time, washed, dressed, hair and teeth brushed, ready for
school as soon as the meal should end. The fruit course
was over, half an orange for each of us, which we ate with
the pointed silver fruit spoons I still have. The maid had
also cleared away the oatmeal. The main course was
before us when Margaret, the eldest of us, spoke up and
said, "How old are you, Daddy?"

Father's deep twinkle flickered at the back of his eyes at
the pert question. "Well, let's see now," he answered in his
slow way. "I can never remember whether I was born in
1871 and married in 1900 or born in 1870 and married in
1901."

This was directed at Mother who was trying to get me to
eat a coddled egg. I loathed coddled eggs.

"Break your toast into it, Elizabeth," she said. And in the
same breath, reprovingly, "We were married in 1901."

"You see?" said Father. "If you'd married me in 1900
when I wanted you to, there wouldn't have been any
confusion." He blew her a kiss which she ignored.

"Did he, Mother? Did he really propose to you a whole
year before you took him?" asked Marg eagerly.

But Mother was too practical for romance at the
breakfast table. "Come along, children," she said. "Finish
your breakfast. It's time to get ready for school."

The break-up of the breakfast circle was a bad moment
for me. It meant that everyone but Mother and me would
disappear for most of the day, and days were long then.
Getting ready for school, at least on a winter day, entailed
a sorting out of mittens and scarves in the coat room under
the hall stairs, and I, unwilling to miss a moment of their
company, would crowd into the tiny room after my sisters,

my efforts to help them causing only delay and confusion. Margaret and Louise, being only one year apart, had matching grey chinchilla cloth coats. I admired them with sinful envy for they had velvet collars.

When the two girls and brother Richard, booted and scarved at last, would march out the front door for that magic place called school, I would say to Mother, "Why can't I go to school?"

"You're too small, dear," she would say. "Maybe next year you can go."

Sometimes, to forestall my whining, Father would say, "Come and drive me as far as Hamilton, Sister." Then, sitting in the driver's seat with me on his lap, he would take off his big driving gauntlets and put them on my hands. Their stiff leather cuffs came almost to my elbows and my fingers had to stretch wide, but I could grasp the wheel well enough to steer down the middle of our empty street. At least I thought I was steering. I'm sure Father's strong hands were there, too. At Hamilton, he would kiss me goodbye and I would run the block and a half home, feeling brave and adventurous and not small at all.

Our house had a Georgian front porch. The wrought iron handrails on either side of the steps ended in two large polished brass balls. Those balls symbolised to me security. So on the mornings when I had to make my own way back from Hamilton, I would run for the sight of the brass balls. Our front door was never locked in the daytime. Pushing through it, I would shout, "I'm home!" and Mother's serene voice would come from somewhere, "All right, dear," and I would know that I was indeed all right.

For a long time after that breakfast table conversation, I pondered the date 1901. I had never before thought of our family as having a beginning. It was just something that had always been. Mother and Father didn't celebrate their wedding anniversary, and as far as I knew, they had been married forever. Now, suddenly, there was a beginning, a definite point in time when our family began. The year 1901 became like The Big Bang in my small cosmos. But what had happened before? What had it been like when I wasn't there?

The story has unfolded piecemeal over many years of pondering and questioning. From Richard I have learned that the years 1900 to 1910 saw Father go from courtship to marriage and the begetting of four children, through four jobs, the building of a new home, and the founding of a business that brought him challenge, excitement, and finally stability.

From Louise I learned that the same decade saw Mother through the transformation from an "old maid" (her own term) of twenty-nine, frustrated in many of her personal ambitions by her father's rigidity, to a wife and mother who was mistress in her own house and adored by a vibrant and ambitious husband.

The two families from which this couple came were quite different in some fundamental ways, though in those late Victorian and early Theodore Roosevelt times the differences were not admitted, nor even recognized. Mother was passionate about her religion. Father was just as passionate about his country. God would take care of the church; he, Father, must cope with this world. These two philosophies, Mother's "love God and thy neighbor," and Father's "God loves those who take care of themselves," were the foundation stones of our upbringing.

When Father set out at age 17 to take up the responsibility to support himself, he was a young man with good health, high ideals, and little money. After a short course at a business college in Minneapolis, he went to Duluth, Minnesota, where some of his older sisters were established. One sunny Sunday afternoon he led his revered sister Lida out to a quiet hillside, seated her upon the grass and told her his great ambition for making the world a better place.

"Young man," said Lida, "you are being sacrilegious! This is God's world. He'll run it a lot better than you can."

Coming down to earth from those Olympian heights, the young man eventually found a job as a cargo broker, locating and arranging cargoes for the long freighters that carried grain from the prairies to the eastern ports and ore from the Minnesota iron ranges to the steel mills of Indiana and Ohio. Full of optimism about the growth of his city, Duluth, he plunged into real estate, buying vacant lots on land contract. Then came the panic of 1893, followed by four years of depression. He could not weather the financial strain and had to declare bankruptcy. It was a bitter lesson, and a blow to his pride, but it taught him much about business cycles. He still had his job, and by frugal living and hard work, he was able to pay off every creditor within the time allowed him and thus save his self-respect. That experience taught him never to invest in real estate that did not produce income. Further, it taught him never to speculate in any commodity. Speculation became a bad word in his economic creed, and he had nothing but contempt for those who made their money simply by playing the stock market. To invest in any enterprise that was producing something of value to society was to invest in America, but to speculate was gambling.

In 1897 he was rooming with a young married couple named Stephenson. In January of that year Mary Stephenson's younger sister, Miss Carrie Louise Beal, of Detroit, came to visit. Inevitably, the two young people, roomer and guest, were thrown together a great deal. He was 26, tall, dark, and extemely handsome; she was 25, petite, vivacious, and beautiful. In the glow of the Stephensons' marital happiness, their friendship ripened apace and might have resulted in an engagement sooner if Father's finances had permitted, but in those days a young man was expected to support the wife of his bosom in the manner to which she was accustomed, and Mother had led a life, not of affluence really, but certainly of economic security.

By 1900 Father's finances were in better shape. He had moved to Evanston, Illinois, to be closer to the Chicago headquarters of the Pittsburgh Steamship Company, a major source of his income. So in April of 1901 the Detroit newspaper carried this quiet announcement:

A very pretty home wedding will be that of
Miss Carrie Beal, daughter of Mr. and Mrs.
William Beal of 39 Charlotte Avenue, and
Mr. Harry Boyd Earhart of Evanston, Illinois,
which will take place on Tuesday next at
five o'clock in the afternoon. Mr. and Mrs
Earhart will make Evanston their home.

This was the beginning, the once-upon-a-time, of our
family story.

41 Charlotte Avenue, c. 1874

CHARLOTTE AVENUE

THE FIRST THREE YEARS were hectic ones with little time to worry about "adjustment." Nine and a half months after the wedding Margaret was born; a year later came Louise; and thirteen months later came Richard. Not until after Richard were the thrice-blessed parents vouchsafed any contraceptive advice. It was a time when the Lord's injunction to Adam and Eve, be fruitful and multiply, was still taken to mean have lots of children. Father's interpretation was, "have as many children as you can support," and three blessed events in 26 months was stretching his economic resources a bit, not to mention Mother's health. Their doctor saw it their way and provided the best advice of the day.

Fortunately for us, both our parents loved babies. When Margaret's first tooth appeared, Mother was so excited she called Father at his office.

"Harry," she cried into the noisy, buzzing instrument that was their only telephone, "the baby has a tooth!"

"Is that you, Carrie? I can hardly hear you," he roared.

"I said the baby has a tooth!"

"What's that? Is something wrong with the baby?"

"No! No! She HAS A TOOTH!"

"Carrie, I can't hear you! Do you want me to come home?"

"NO! Oh, NO! I'm just telling you Margaret has a TOOTH."

Such were the excitements that filled Mother's days as Margaret, then Louise, then Richard arrived, one after the other. Father shared her fascination with them. It was he who walked the floor nights when Margaret was teething, so Mother in her new pregnancy could get some sleep. He would croon over and over, "You little tycoon/You awake too soon." But the increasing family meant increasing pressure on him to provide for them.When the United States Steel Company bought the Pittsburgh Steamship

Company, he felt that too much power was suddenly concentrated in the hands of one man in Cleveland, and the future of his own job looked less certain. Hearing of an opening at the Russell Wheel and Foundry Company in Detroit for a young man who could design and sell logging machinery, he went off to investigate, got the job and found a place for his family to live.

In May of 1904, when Richard was only six weeks old, Father sent for his family to join him. Mother had to bring the three babies by train, a long, tedious, dirty, lonesome ride through the blossoming fruit orchards of southern Michigan. It was an exhausting trip, but Mother was buoyed by her anticipation of things to come, for they were to live for a time in her own old home, the house where she had been born. Father would be waiting for her and they would drive through the dear familiar streets. Perhaps Grandfather would lend the Beal carriage for the occasion, since it was to meet his own granchildren.

Father did indeed meet her, strong, vital, exuberant Father, but to her dismay, he led her with obvious pride, not to the comfortable family carriage, but to one of those frightening, new-fangled automobiles! Poor tired Mother could only say, "Oh, Harry! Is it safe?"

Mother's birthplace was an old, white frame farmhouse at 41 Charlotte Avenue. It had survived the change in neighborhood from farm land to city street, keeping only its large garden and raspberry patch. The houses were not even numbered when Grandfather bought the place soon after the Civil War, but eventually number 41 had acquired the amenities of the time—electricity, indoor plumbing, even a telephone on the wall in the front hall. Before either of his daughters had married, Grandfather had built a larger, more substantial house where his raspberry patch had been. So Mother was coming back to the house of her beginning, this time as its mistress, bringing with her a husband and three children. She was an adult now and no longer subject to her ailing and domineering father, but comforted by being next door to the saintly mother she adored. Her old church welcomed her, and so did a large circle of devoted friends. The choir in which she had sung as a girl had missed her voice and were eager to have her back. Her Sunday School class of little boys, now three years older, remembered her with affection—was she going to teach them again? The Women's Foreign Missionary Society needed her. Zetema, a women's literary society in which she had been active before her marriage, made her an honorary member. This gave her the privilege of attending meetings where she saw many of her best friends, but without the responsibility of preparing papers for their discussions. All of these activities she loved, for she was gregarious by nature, but her chief concern was for her family.

Three active babies kept life from being dull. On one day it was Richard who was almost run over by a runaway horse in the alley behind the house. On another day Margaret, hearing the cry of the fruit vendor as he came down the block calling, "Strawberries...Strawberries" mimicked him with, "tawbe'ies...tawbe'ies," which brought the man to the door expecting a sale. He was irate at what he took for mockery from a rude brat, and Mother had trouble placating his Italian temper without buying the strawberries she didn't want.

While the neighbors were for the most part friendly and helpful, there came a day when she found their interest a bit more than she had bargained for. She was playing with Richard in the living room when the doorbell rang. Richard had been fussy of late, though for the most part he was a chubby, healthy baby. He followed Mother to the door in a happy mood, clinging to her skirts and peering roguishly from their safety at the strange woman who stood there.

"Are you the lady of the house?" asked the apparition.

"Yes," said Mother.

"And is your name..." she consulted a list, "Mrs. Earhart?"

"Yes," assented Mother, puzzled.

"Well, Mrs. Earhart, I'm from the Society For The Prevention of Cruelty to Children, and I have been requested by one of your neighbors to investigate why your little boy cries so much."

Mother was caught between laughter and outrage, but recognizing the dilemma of a social worker who has been sent on a silly errand, she decided on laughter. "Well, here he is," she said. "You're welcome to look him over for bruises if you like."

Richard clung closer and buried his face in the voluminous skirt that was his refuge.

"Oh, dear no!" said the Angel of Mercy. "I'm sure there's been some mistake!" and with that, she fled.

In 1903, back in Pennsylvania, Grandma Earhart died. She had been a strong and tender woman whose courage and idealism had bound all her children to her in loyalty and devotion. Grandpa was dependent on her. Now he was cut adrift from his anchor and took refuge with one or another of his children until Father and Mother offered him a permanent home with us in 1906. Mother had always stood in awe of the capable and aggressive Earhart sisters, not only for their academic accomplishments some of which far exceeded hers, but for their practical knowledge of affairs domestic.

"When I was engaged," she told me once, "and Grandma Earhart came for the wedding, we were invited to a luncheon at a friend's house. As we stood in the hallway, we could smell something delicious frying in the kitchen, and Grandma turned to me and whispered, 'She's using half drippings and half lard!' How could I ever match that kind of knowledge?"

As to the sisters, Aunt Lida, the erudite Aunt Lida who had a Ph.D. from Columbia and had taught at Teachers' College there, offered to help Mother hem the linen table napkins which were so necessary a part of every girl's trousseau and which must be hemmed by hand. Aunt Lida took two dozen, "And when they came back" said Mother enviously, "all beautifully laundered, of course, not one stitch could I see!" Perhaps it was this envy of her sisters-in-laws' skill at needlework that made Mother hide away a handmade quilt which was probably an engagement or a wedding present from one of them. Or perhaps quilts seemed too countrified for the elegant living she aspired to. At any rate, I found it many years later, unused, in a chest in the servants' wing of the big house when I was helping to close up the place after Father died. For several years I used it as the spread on my own bed. Joan has it now and displays it with pride on the wall of her guest room. Quilts are back in style.

When the father of the accomplished Earhart sisters became a member of her own family circle, Mother found that it was not unalloyed pleasure to have him around all the time. He was devoted to us children, spoiled us, made things for us at his work bench in the basement, and put up with our pranks, but his constant presence, particularly at meal times, was a strain on her. She couldn't correct our manners without an implied criticism of his, and his were different. His "hearing aid" was a large black ear trumpet. During meals it rested by his side until he was addressed directly. Then he would lay down his fork, insert the trumpet in one ear or the other, for he was deaf in both, and re-join the banter and confusion of the family circle. Since he had not heard a word of what had gone before, this did not make for light repartee. Besides, his false teeth didn't fit, and their clickety-clack as he chewed formed a continuous obligato to the general conversation.

I never knew the real cause of his departure from our household. He was eighty years old and perhaps needed more care than Mother could give him, or perhaps he needed more peace than we children gave him. Be that as it may, I lost a good friend when he left us. In 1914 he went to Duluth to live with his daughter, Josephine Hunter.

In the early days of the family's Detroit life, Father's job required a great deal of travel. As the southern pine lands took over from the depleted Michigan forests, the demands for logging machinery came more and more from the South, and Father traveled many a mile to make sure it was his company's product that satisfied that demand.

He was not one to sit back and wait when opportunity beckoned. Once, coming back from such a trip, he had a connection to make in Buffalo. The train he was on was running later by the hour, and he became more and more worried lest he miss that connection. It would make a twelve hour difference to him, and he had an important appointment in Detroit for the next day. Summoning the conductor, he handed him a telegram form and said, "I'd like this message sent to the New York Central station master at Buffalo."

The conductor looked at the message. It said simply, "Hold #17 for Earhart."

"How do you want it signed?" he asked.

"You sign it," said Father.

"I can't do that," said the conductor, aghast. "I don't even know who this Earhart is."

"Never mind," said Father. "For all the station master knows, Earhart is a vice president of the New York Central. You just send that telegram from you, and..." handing him a generous bill, "keep the change."

The message was sent. Number 17 waited. Earhart made his appointment in Detroit.

The panic of 1907 came and went. Father's bitter experience with the one in '93 may have kept him from disaster a second time for he did manage to keep his head above water, but his job at Russell Wheel and Foundry ended in a dispute over policy, and his next job at Detroit Hoist and Machine eventually ended the same way. Never a patient man, he may have had a few things to learn about tact in those early encounters with entrenched authority. Whether these partings were voluntary or otherwise he never discussed in later years, even with Richard. Mother backed him loyally through the changes and never lost her faith in him. Her social position gave him some status and a firm base from which to rise, but it was his own drive and perspicacity that brought him up in the world.

After leaving Detroit Hoist and Machine, about the year 1909, he became agent for a small company called the White Star Refining Company of Buffalo. It had but one other agent, a man in Cleveland. Father was soon dissatisfied with the way things were run, for the company was losing money and the Buffalo office was doing nothing about it. He saw that with the demand for automobiles growing, the demand for motor oils ought to be growing, too. In 1911 he bought the trademarks, formulae, and goodwill of the faltering company and established the White Star Refining Company of Michigan. Detroit at that time was a town of about 300,000, a middle class, middle western city largely contained within the Grand Boulevard which swept around it in an arc with a radius of about three miles. To the south, the Detroit River subtended the arc and formed the border with Canada. (Detroit is still the only place in the U.S. which looks south to Canada.) Jefferson Avenue ran more or less parallel to the river, and White Star's first office was at the corner of West Jefferson and Dry Dock Street. It was a one-story, two room, cinder block building. There Father reigned as president, secretary, bookkeeper, salesman, and janitor. His salary was $150 a month. His staff consisted of himself and one man, a chemist to blend the oils.

Those were the gory, glory days of John D. Rockefeller's thrust for monopoly. Competition among the big oil companies was utterly ruthless and too often unscrupulous. Someone who knew Father remarked to a friend of Mother's, "I hear young Harry Earhart is going into the oil business. Too bad! You can't succeed in that game and be honest very long."

Father's reaction when he heard it was a grim, "We'll see about that!"

By the end of the first year, sales had reached the $50,000 mark. Seventeen years later there were 1,000 employees and the yearly volume had reached $20,000,000. It took no more than a handshake to seal a contract then, for the petroleum industry knew that Harry Earhart's integrity was unimpeachable.

At first, White Star's business was a compounding operation, blending and selling lubricants, greases, cutting oils and even soap, but not gasoline. Until World War I gasoline was sold at hardware stores, almost as a by-product of kerosene. When service stations came into being just before the war, White Star bought a chain called Economy Stations, where they sold fuel oil for industry and shipping, as well as gasoline to the public. By 1917, the government was already regulating crude oil distribution. In order to get any allocation at all, White Star had to do its own refining. Therefore, the company bought a small refinery in Oklahoma, then the tank cars for shipping its products north.

So intense was the competition during that hectic time that, in order to keep the cars from being hijacked, White Star had to put a man on board to ride them down to the field empty and back full. That man, Harry Howard, was a gentleman of some resource. Once when he was under pressure to get a shipment back to Detroit to meet a contract date, he got his tank cars hitched to an express train. It was an unheard of feat, for express trains, which had priority along those busy rails over everything but the fast passenger trains, were not supposed to haul freight. That was the kind of initiative and enterprise that gave zest to the competition Father loved.

As the demand for gasoline grew, White Star needed more stations. To finance the expansion, Father applied to the Dime Savings Bank of Detroit for a loan. The loan officer turned him down. Undaunted, Father went to the bank's president. ("Always go to the top" was one of his maxims, one of the many he borrowed from his hero, Theodore Roosevelt.) The president was "Sailor Bill" Livingstone, a man with whose family Mother had grown up.

"Mr. Livingstone," said Father respectfully, "your loan officer does not see eye to eye with me about a loan I applied for, but I think he has overlooked some important considerations. I think the expansion I contemplate will be important to the city of Detroit and could have a very beneficial effect on your bank's business. I would like the privilege of presenting my case to your Board of Directors myself."

Mr. Livingstone, with a twinkle, said, "If Carrie Beal can trust you, I guess I can. Come and tell us about it."

The board listened. The board granted the loan!

Part II

1910-1920

VIRGINIA PARK

SHORTLY AFTER Mother's sister Mary married Jack Stephenson and moved to Duluth, Grandfather Beal gave them $10,000 to build a house. About 1906 or 1907 he did the same for Mother and Father. With that modest sum they built a comfortable brick house of twelve rooms with a large attic and a full basement on Virginia Avenue.

Virginia Avenue was a new street in 1908. Its three blocks, extending from Woodward Avenue on the east to Hamilton on the west, were paved with hexagonal cedar blocks. Beyond Hamilton it was a sea of black mud. Ours was only the third house built in the middle block.

"Why must you go so far out in the country?" asked Mother's friends. "Virginia Avenue must be way out. It's beyond Grand Boulevard, isn't it?"

"Only six blocks," Mother would reply, "and the streetcars run right down Woodward Avenue so it will be easy to get to church. We'll be only a block from Woodward, you know."

By the spring of 1908 the family had moved in, and by the winter of 1909 I, the fourth baby, had arrived. I was born at home on a February morning in the big mahogany sleigh bed that had been Grandmother Beal's. Mother's and Father's bedroom was at one front corner of the house on the second floor and my sisters' room was at the other. They were connected by the bathroom the girls shared with Mother. When Father went in to waken the girls for breakfast on that momentous morning, Margaret was already sitting up, too excited to mind the cold.

"What is it, Daddy?" she asked, bouncing up and down.

Father went about his usual routine of closing windows as though it was just any morning. He pulled the fallen covers back over the recumbent Louise.

"What's what?" he countered.

"What's the baby, a boy or girl?"

"What baby?" teased Father.

"Daddy! We know the baby came last night because we heard it crying. Is it a boy or a girl?"

"Oh, you must have heard a puppy dog crying," said Father, a bit fey after the night's ordeal.

"Dad-ee!"

"Well, Honey Bunch," he relented, "you have a new baby sister, a fine healthy little girl. Come on, Weezy, wake up. You girls must get ready for breakfast by yourselves this morning. The Little Mother and the baby are sleeping. Perhaps after breakfast you can come in and see them." Then he went to break the great news to Richard. Richard, not quite five, was taken wholly by surprise. Nobody had ever told him Mother was going to have a baby! Why didn't she get another boy?

This story, naturally, became one of my favorites. Its frequent repetition and the chuckles that went with it easily convinced me that my arrival was a happy event. I was a mother myself before I ever realized that it was indubitably an unplanned one. But, planned or not, never did I feel unwanted. Each of us had a secure place in the family circle. Margaret was The Brain. Her quick wit, curiosity, vivid imagination, and sense of humor, as well as her seniority, made her our leader. Louise, with her black hair, deep brown eyes—the only one of us to have Father's eyes—with her straight nose and slender figure, was The Beauty. Dick, the only son, who had to bear all the burdens of chivalry in a bevy of sisters and yet be the athlete and sportsman, was The Boy. I, spoiled, petted, loved, teased, and protected, was The Baby.

The year 1909 was a wonderful time to be born. I came into an expanding world. Automobiles, flying machines, telephones, moving pictures, electricity for lighting homes—all those things still had an aura of wonder about them, and as I grew I was witness to their evolution from miracles to necessities. Of course I didn't know I was watching evolution, but Father knew. He believed with no shadow of doubt that only in the United States of America could this amazing explosion of science and invention have taken place. Mother, who valued "brotherly love" more than new inventions, was not sure that competition was the highest motivation for good Christians, but to Father there was no conflict between brotherly love and brotherly competition. The Great Free Competitive American Enterprise System was what had spawned this explosion of inventiveness and made America the greatest nation in history. That was God's will as he saw it, and he rejoiced to be a part of it.

The Virginia Park of my childhood evokes happy memories. It was a pleasant street, elm-shaded and brick-paved by the time I knew it. Brick gateways at Woodward and at Hamilton had transformed it from Virginia Avenue to Virginia Park. On sunny days an Italian flower vendor would push his two-wheeled cart through our block, calling his wares and finding an eager customer in Mother.

In the heat of summer, there was a water wagon to wash the street. A team of horses pulled the wagon bearing a huge tank from which sprang a gentle shower of cool water. We would run along beside it, bare-footed and shouting with joy, while the driver aloft on his hard bench ignored us disdainfully.

Horses pulled most of the service vehicles. In hot weather they wore straw hats with holes cut through for their ears. The patient beasts plodded along, their tails switching constantly at the pestilential flies while the drivers sat somnolently under large, multi-colored umbrellas.

The tar wagon for street repair was another delight. When it came to our neighborhood, we would gather around it, half fascinated, half repelled. The hissing flame that kept the tar flowing was frightening, but the glossy black fluid itself had a certain beauty that overcame the repugnant smell. Besides, he who could dip a finger in the mess and withdraw a glob without getting burned was a hero.

"Chew some," said my friends. "Here's some that's not too hot. Chew it. It'll make your teeth white."

"Ugh! No!" I hated the stuff.

When the ice wagon came, we children would cluster

around to catch the chips as the friendly ice man shaped his big blocks to fit individual ice boxes.

Because of all the horses, there had to be the White Wing Squad, white-coated men with long-handled brooms and pans who swept up the manure and dropped it into two-wheeled barrels. I ran along beside them with my friends, chorusing the expected pee-ew, but secretly rather liking the smell.

The Merchants Delivery wagons brought all sorts of parcels and supplies. Groceries, milk, ice—all such household necessities came right to the door, but if the need arose for something special, a Lady Baltimore cake, say, to dress up a dull dessert, or some individual Charlotte Russes, there was a bakery just a couple of blocks away on Woodward. Right next to it was Simons & Cooper, the drugstore where ice cream sodas went for a nickel and the lime drops were so good. For medicines, there was Meade's Drugstore a few blocks in the other direction on Hamilton. Demery's for dry goods was on Woodward near Grand Boulevard. To all of these we walked.

Occasionally, Mother would take us farther afield on the streetcar, downtown to Newcomb Endicott, our largest department store, or to R.H. Fyfe's for shoes. She had Louise with her one day in Newcomb's, forerunner of the J. L. Hudson Company which is now a part of Dayton-Hudson. As they stepped into the elevator, there was only one other passenger, a pleasant looking lady who smiled rather diffidently at them. Mother knew the face was familiar but was at a loss for the woman's name. After a moment, as their iron cage bore them slowly upward, she confessed, "I'd like so much to introduce my daughter to you, but I'm embarrassed to say I can't remember your name."

The lady bowed kindly, "I'm Mrs. Henry Ford, " she said!

Streetcar rides were fraught with certain perils, among them the possibility of carsickness. There was a good deal of sway to the lumbering old cars, especially if the run was long enough to get up speed. Then Mother, looking down at our unhappy faces, would draw from her capacious

pocketbook (her "portmanteau" or her "reticule" in
Father's heavy parlance) a package of gum. Margaret,
Louise, and Richard each got a whole piece. I got half a
piece, along with the unfailing admonition, "You musn't
swallow it, Elizabeth. Remember?" Then Margaret would
repeat the warning, and presently Dick would chime in
with, "Swallowed it yet, Eliz?" and I, disappointed over
the half piece, annoyed by the advice and angry over the
teasing, would chew on in sulky silence, hoping only that
the end of the ride would come before I really was sick.

Streetcars were the chief vehicles of public transport.
The old horse-drawn cars of Mother's day had given way
to the electric ones by my time, but a few of the open-sided
ones survived for warm weather use. The dangerous
practice by some daring souls of jumping on or off while
the car was in motion, or perhaps the number of fares so
evaded, finally put those cars, too, out of business.

The overhead trolley wires were centered above our
main avenues, and the tracks perforce ran beneath them.
The cars had to pick up and discharge passengers in the
middle of the street. Mother was driving her Churchill
Electric down Woodward Avenue one day when a
passenger, not wary enough, stepped off the streetcar and
started for the curb without looking. Those old electrics
were not built for quick stops. Mother could not avoid the
woman, knocked her down, and ran over her shoulder.
The woman recovered, but Mother never got over the
shock and refused to drive for many years thereafter.

Longer trips, such as those to picnics on Belle Isle, we
took in our Chalmers 30 touring car with Father at the
wheel. Mother sat in front beside Father in a state of
perpetual terror, and the four of us were piled into the
back with no more squabbling over who got the outside
seats than usually occurs in families. No less either. It was
inevitably my fate to get the "telephone chair," a low chair
requisitioned from its place on the stair landing by the
telephone and set sideways between the front and back
seats. There were no jump seats in the old Chalmers.

Our route took us down Woodward Avenue to the
Grand Boulevard, that busy intersection where, years

later, traffic lights were first introduced to the world. At the time, there was just a lone policeman standing in the middle of things with a whistle and his two hands to control the traffic's flow. At the Boulevard, we turned left and followed its arc to the river, there to cross the bridge to our lovely city park. No milling crowds disturbed the quiet in those days. Families like ours settled themselves on the grass with much open space between them. Weeping willows draped their veils in the river, graceful streamers that swayed in the swells from the long ships passing. Here we would take off our shoes and wade, or run through the lush grass while Mother spread a cloth under our favorite tree and prepared our feast. Devilled eggs we had, and sandwiches with homemade bread, fruit and cookies or cake for dessert, with lemonade or milk to drink. No bananas, though. Mother denied us those, either because Richard had once eaten some that were too green and been sick or because she was afraid of finding a tarantula hiding in a bunch from the grocery store as her mother had sometimes done.

On such a picnic when I was about three, we young ones were wading happily under the willows. I spied a pretty stone and, after the manner of three-year-olds, I squatted instead of leaning over to pick it up. The cries of warning from my peers neither enlightened nor deterred me. I emerged with my prize but with wet pants, and was roundly scolded by my self-appointed guardians. Mother, all unperturbed, said, "Don't fuss, children. You go and climb trees while Elizabeth lies here in the sun. It will soon dry her rompers." Next to wading, tree climbing was my favorite outdoor sport, so lying prone in the sun was more punishment than I felt I deserved.

The Chalmers was our first gasoline-driven car. Before that we had two electrics: a Phipps-Grinnell first, then a Churchill, both built like square, plate glass goldfish bowls set on shiny black chassis. They had soft seats upholstered in grey plush and cut-glass flower vases affixed beside the driver. Both were quiet, demure, and elegant. But they were ponderous creations and undependable, for their enormous batteries required frequent charging. One evening as Father and Mother were returning from a formal dress affair down town, those batteries failed them just where the viaduct on Cass Avenue dips under the railroad tracks. They coasted down the slope, but there was not enough "juice" to get them up the farther side. Father had to get out in his dress suit, high silk hat and all, and push the monster up to the level street! Is it any wonder he switched to gasoline-fueled cars?

When Dick was about ten, Father replaced the Chalmers with a Studebaker. To Mother's consternation the new car arrived in the daytime while Father was at the office. She dispatched Richard to the garage to receive the salesman's instructions. Richard, like most boys of his age and time, was fascinated by automobiles. It all looked so easy to him, he must needs try out the instructions for himself when the salesman had departed. The result was unexpectedly successful. The car shot backwards out of the garage, startling Dick and paralysing Mother who was watching from the safety of the kitchen window.

"Richard!" she scolded. "Get out of that car and come in here this instant. You must never do such a thing again. You are a very naughty boy. When your father comes home and hears about this, he will certainly give you a good spanking!"

But when Father came home and repaired quickly to the garage to see his new toy, he was completely baffled by it. After struggling with the meager written instructions and his own limited knowledge of how an internal combustion engine is supposed to work, he had to send for Richard.

"What in blazes am I doing wrong?" he fumed.

Richard showed him. Whereupon, of course, his respect for his son's superior knowledge precluded any thought of the promised spanking!

PASTIMES

I THINK OF THAT decade of the teens—and it encompassed my earliest memories—as a happy time. Mother sang as she went about her housewifely affairs. I remember trying to imitate the scuff of her feet as she ran up the stairs. She always ran. Sometimes she would sit at the upright piano and teach me nursery songs from a book with enchanting pictures. Much of the time she left me to my own devices, secure in the knowledge I would not stray too far. I played games of my own imagining on the oriental rug that covered our living room floor, the rug my daughter Joan has now. In the sunny south window Grandpa Earhart sat most mornings while he lived with us, his big leather platform rocker squeaking companionably as he read the morning paper. His deafness walled him in so completely that he could not hear me as I sneaked up to him and, with a loud BOO! punched in his barricade. I thought this was a dandy game, for he always responded with a laugh. Then he would take me up on his knee and rock me as we talked with the aid of his ear trumpet. If there was an apple handy, he would take out his penknife and carefully, carefully peel it so the skin came off paper thin and in one unbroken spiral. He was a great believer in fruit. He taught me to save peach pits. The one we planted together in the garden beside the sandbox, in time actually grew into a peach tree—MY peach tree.

For me, the big excitement of the day was when my sisters and brother came home from school. Then the games took on more life. While I was still small enough to be called "the Baby," which means before I was six, I had a friend who lived in the same block, Doris Douglas by name. Margaret and Louise used to dress the two of us up in their own long nightgowns and crowd us into their doll carriages to wheel us up and down Virginia Park in mock maternity. Alas for me! Our two mothers would fight over which one was to have Doris, for Doris had naturally curly hair!

At age six, I rebelled. I was in the kitchen with Mother one day when Dick came home from school. In passing through, he called me Babe. I stamped my foot and turned to Mother.

"I'm NOT a baby," I said. "I don't want to be called Babe!"

"Of course you don't," said Mother. "It's time to stop that." And stop it she did. No one ever called me Babe or so referred to me again, at least not in my hearing.

Margaret had no such champion when some of the neighborhood boys got hold of Father's pet name for her, Honey Bunch. They surrounded her with delighted taunts. "Oh, Honey Bunch!" "Look over here, Honey Bunch." "Come on, Honey Bunch. I dare you!" Marg took after them in fury. As Dick said, "She was fighting mad and was ready to take on all the boys on Virginia Park and clean house with them!" They fled from her attack.

Louise, too, had a temper. Her dark eyes would flash and her tongue could scorch when she was aroused. She has said that growing up between Margaret and Richard squashed her ego, yet one day when Richard cornered her in his teasing, she slashed her doll across his face, breaking the doll and giving him a cut that scarred him for life. Richard went howling to Mother and Louise fled sobbing to her room, her ego bruised perhaps by remorse, but far from dead. One of her more daring exploits was to go down the clothes chute.

Our clothes chute was of generous size, descending from an opening at chair height in the second floor bathroom to the cement floor of the basement, and Louise, remembering how the firemen at the fire station around the corner slid down their polished pole, decided to try the quick route. By bracing arms and knees against the sides, she managed miraculously to reach the bottom without broken bones.

Mother promptly had a bar put across the top opening.

Heights appealed to us, possibly because Detroit was so flat. My friend Doris and I were about nine or ten when we learned about parachutes, and the idea of floating gently earthward from an airplane had all the appeal of an Arabian Nights tale. We took an umbrella from the stand in the front hall and climbed to our third floor playroom. As she opened the "parachute" outside the south window, Doris drew back.

"I don't know, Liz. That looks scary."

"Oh, go on. It will be just like the Magic Carpet," I assured her. "Here, let me try."

I took the umbrella from her, but fortunately my nerve, too, failed when I looked down to the back porch so far below. "Maybe we'd better not," I said lamely.

That playroom was a glorious big empty room on the top floor. When plans for the house were being drawn, that's where Father insisted it should be. "I'm not going to have my kiddies relegated to a dark basement for their play space," said he. "They shall have light and air." (I doubt if he had parachutes in mind.)

The room had dormer windows, which gave each of us a niche for our special possessions but left ample room for action—for plays, even for roller skating on rainy days. It was a room where we were allowed great freedom for creativity. I did a lot of reading up there, puzzling out the words I didn't know and interrupting Marg's writing to help me with the hardest ones.

Marg's writing often took the form of plays which were acted out in that playroom with a cast recruited from the neighborhood. I was usually posted at the head of the stairs to collect admission, two pins, from the faithful parents who attended.

Though Marg was a prolific playwright, few of her masterpieces have survived. During the summer we spent at Bay View, she wrote one in verse based on one of Father's homilies called The Little Boy Who Wanted the Moon. I don't remember the plot, but two deathless lines were cherished for years in the family's anthology of our youthful sayings. They were spoken by the MEAN OLD WOMAN (Louise) when her POOR LITTLE SLAVY (Richard) was about to be released from her clutches:

Willie, Willie, don't forget
I took you in when you were wet!

Other memorable things happened that summer at Bay
View. The year was 1914. Dick marked it as the summer
World War I began; I mark it as the summer I learned
about onions. I came home from playschool one day and
found Dick in the kitchen where a bunch of beautiful big
fresh green ones had just arrived from the market garden
nearby. Dick liked them, but I distrusted anything I had
never tasted. Dick was munching one with obvious
enjoyment, and I was hungry.

"Can I have one?" I asked doubtfully.

"Sure. Help yourself."

"Will I like it?"

"Try one. They're good."

"How do you eat them?"

"Just put it in your mouth and bite."

I crammed the whole thing in at once and bit as I was
told, with a result that nearly took the top of my skull off.
To make it worse, the slippery thing was too big to come
out. I wailed; Dick chortled; Mother came running; Dick
got spanked for teasing his little sister. Poor Dick!

A few cottages away from ours that summer stood that
of the Hendrickson family. Mrs. Hendrickson, a widow
and a long time friend of Mother's, had three daughters.
The youngest, Virginia, was just Dick's age. Their cottage
had fascinating angles and gables, all encrusted with fancy
Victorian "gingerbread," and its many porches had sloping
or peaked roofs where we children had been strictly
forbidden to climb. However, some temptations are too
great to resist. There came a day when Dick, emulating
Stout Cortez who "stared with eagle eyes at the
Pacific...silent upon a peak in Darien," stood on one of
those peaked roofs and stared with eagle eyes out over
Little Traverse Bay. He had Ginny Hendrickson beside
him. Ginny, less sure-footed than he, began to slide off.
Dick reached out a hand and managed to forestall
disaster.

Virginia's mother was almost tearful in her gratitude

when she heard about it. The next day she came to thank Mother for Richard's heroism. "He saved Virginia's life, Carrie!" But Mother took a different view. Richard got another spanking for having disobeyed orders. Life was indeed hard for Richard.

Margaret's vivid imagination kept us supplied with stories and plays, but was not limited to her writing. The summer we spent down the river at Grosse Isle, she and I both had imaginary playmates. Mine was Rose. Rose and I carried on long, secret conversations on an imaginary telephone of Marg's devising. The real telephone in that cottage was on a rural party line. Affixed to the wall, it had a little crank to actuate the bell. Each party on the line had a different pattern of ring, so one could "ring up" a neighbor without the aid of Central, simply by imitating his pattern - two short and one long, or whatever. Our imaginary telephones were outside, Marg's at one telephone pole and mine at another. By putting an ear to the pole one could hear the hum of wires overhead. This meant the line was clear. Then by rapping out a secret "ring" against the pole, I could get Rose or Marg could get her friend. Alas, when we compared notes afterwards, which was part of the game, Marg's friend had always said much more interesting things than Rose had! That summer Marg and I rode broomstick horses, fashioned elaborate stables for them from old crates and straw, and tamed the wild and rearing creatures with consummate, if imaginary, skill. All this training in imaginative play had much to do with my adjustment to a lonelier life when Margaret, Louise, and Dick went away to school.

Different sports marked the seasons. Winter brought clean, white snow for the snow forts we armed with the hardest snowballs possible. Teams of our neighborhood gang fought royal battles with great inaccuracy of aim but with fervor as long as the ammunition lasted. Or when there was a fresh fall, we would trample out a great circle on its pristine whiteness for a game of fox-and-geese. Do children still play fox-and-geese, I wonder? I can almost feel now the bite of the frosty air as we raced madly around that circle trying to elude the fox.

"Dick, you be the fox. You're the fastest."

"Heck, no! I'm always the fox."

"Okay. Then we'll count out."

So we would line up with mittened fists held out in front of us, and someone, perhaps Marg, would intone as she touched each fist in turn.

> "Ibbety, bibbety, sibbety, sab.
> Ibbety, bibbety, knabe."

Knabe was the fox. What made the game so exciting was that whenever the fox tagged a goose, that goose became the fox and the fox became a goose. Keeping track of who was predator and who was game, kept minds as active as legs.

We had a wooden toboggan slide that fitted over our back steps. This we iced by pouring boiling water over it, the quaint theory being that hot water froze faster than cold. It wasn't much of a hill, but it was all we had and we enjoyed it.

Sometimes there were expeditions out North Woodward to Palmer Park (always pronounced Parmer Park) for ice skating. Skates then had clamps and straps to fasten them to one's everyday shoes. If the high buttoned shoes were tight enough to give support, they were all right, but the laced up ones were better. It didn't matter much to me because my skates had double runners and I could have worn them over just stockings if it had not been for the cold. I was never a success on ice.

Spring called forth roller skates, jumping ropes, hoops rescued from discarded barrels, and those precursors of the skateboard which we called scooters. We built these last ourselves by nailing half a roller skate to each end of a sturdy board, and an apple crate or some other firm wooden box upright at the front. A stick fastened across the top of the box served for handlebars. We propelled the contraption with one foot on the board and one outboard, hands clutching the handlebar for balance and for steering. When we played Merchants Delivery, scooters were our trucks.

FAMILY CIRCLE

THOUGH OUR DAYTIME lives were separate because we went to different schools and had different playmates, we came together as a family in the evenings. The high point of the day was Father's homecoming. We were back in the house by then, and when we heard his car in the driveway, we would swarm out the back door to fall upon him as he emerged from the garage, carrying his briefcase ("wallet" to him) heavy with the evening's homework. Then would follow a ritual at the tall rope swing Grandpa had built for us. Our weary parent would push one after the other of us skyward, each would jump off at the highest point to yield to the next. I was last, of course, and because I was too timid to jump, I had to "let the old cat die." "Wait! Wait for me!" I would screech as they gamboled off towards dinner.

At evening the house embraced us. The French doors where we entered from the back yard opened into our living room. It was a long room, not quite wide enough for good proportions. Midway of the east wall, to our right as we came in, was a generous fireplace with brass andirons and a brass fender. Its hearth and facing were of soft green tile. The mantel was just the right height for hanging our stockings on Christmas Eve, and my faith that Santa Claus came down our chimney on his magic rounds was unshakeable, because Margaret had actually heard him trip over the fender one year. Who could argue against evidence like that?

The long bookcases flanking the fireplace held wondrous things behind their glass doors: whole sets of books like *The Young Folks Library* and *The Book of Knowledge*, story books like *Tanglewood Tales* and *The Arabian Nights*, *Grimm's Fairy Tales* and Hans Christian Andersen's, as well as duller things for older readers. A reading lamp with a Tiffany shade representing an apple tree in blossom stood on a table nearby, and Mother's carriage clock twirled its pendulum silently under a glass bell on the mantel.

Here in this room of warmth and comfort, Mother would be waiting to give Father his homecoming kiss and send us all off to wash before dinner.

Opposite the fireplace was the doorway to the hall, hung with velvet portieres which served admirably as stage curtains when we put on one of Margaret's plays. The hall, like the living room, ran the depth of the house. At the back end a central stairway rose gracefully to a landing where a tall Palladian window gave light to the halls, both upstairs and down. The stairway divided and turned back on either side. The stair carpet was grass green, a continuous runner whose every step was anchored by a polished brass stair rod. Under the landing on one side was a small lavatory where we "made our ablutions," to use Father's phrase; on the other side was the coat closet.

The dining room was across the hall from the living room. The sight of Mother's silver, some of which I still use, brings back vivid pictures of it. The big bay window to the west looked directly into Mrs. Zaccharius's kitchen. An oak sideboard stood against the south wall, and a Tiffany lamp hung over the round oak table. There was always a white linen table cloth for dinner. Each water glass stood at the tip of each knife on the right; each butter plate with its little butter spreader beside it at the tip of each fork on the left. Our napkins lay neatly rolled in our individual napkin rings beside the forks. We had butter balls in those days, and when hunger overcame me before dinner was ready, I sometimes sneaked between the closed portieres and ate my butter ball whole. In fact, I did not always stop with my own. Mother adroitly cured me of this habit by teaching me to use the corrugated wooden paddles to make the butter balls for all. I became frugal with butter very quickly.

When the maid or butler, depending on whether we had two "girls" or a married couple, pushed back the portieres and announced dinner, we would all troop in and take our places. Father would pull out Mother's chair for her first. She sat at the north side where she could keep an eye on the pantry door and summon the maid by the buzzer under

her foot. To her right sat Margaret, then Louise, then
Father opposite Mother, with the serving dishes arrayed
in front of him. To his right came Richard, and I closed the
circle.

No meal began without grace. We knew Mother's by
heart for it was always the same:

> Oh Lord, bless this food prepared for our use
> and our lives to Thy service, in Jesus' name,
>   Amen.

Father's were of unpredictable length, either a
spontaneous prayer of gratitude or a particularly reverent
grace he had come across in his reading.

Father's carving was deft, and he was proud of it. It was
part of the nightly show to watch him draw his big carving
knife across the steel sharpener with a flourish worthy of
Cyrano de Bergerac. He stood up to slice the roast or
disjoint the fowl while the maid waited to pass around the
plates. If we had chicken he needed no extra tools, but if it
happened to be duck he had to carve, he called for his
special "clippers." These he used with the precision of a
surgeon to divide the succulent bird into portions he
thought appropriate to each appetite. His servings were
generous, especially with the gravy. He used the round
gravy ladle to make little wells in our mashed potatoes and
filled them to overflowing. As a special treat when we had
roast beef, he would soak our bread in the plate gravy.
Every bite was supposed to "go down the little red lane,"
and if the serving was more than we wanted, or if the
vegetable was unpopular, we were adjured to "remember
the starving Armenians" for whose sake we must eat every
mouthful. I never understood the logic of this, but as none
of the rest of my generation did either, I let it pass.

When our verbal exchanges, call it bickering if you will,
got too noisy, either Mother or Father would quell us with:

> We will fold our hands together.
> We will sit up straight together.
> We will mind the rule of Sunday School

And all be still together.

Oıder restored, a game of some sort would follow, a spelling game like ghosts, or a guessing game like twenty questions, or a geography game. Games kept the conversation general and under control, not to mention sharpening wits.

In front of the dining room and overlooking the street was a small den where Mother had her big mahogany dropfront desk and Father his leather couch. After dinner, while the others read or did homework, Father would often read aloud to me there. To his mind no stories ever equaled the remembered ones from his *McGuffey's Fourth Reader*, but his renditions of the Thornton Burgess *Old Mother West Wind* series, or the *Hollow Tree Books*, or *Mrs. Wiggs of the Cabbage Patch* illumined those for me. He read beautifully, slowly and with fine expression, but not even he could arouse my interest in *Alice In Wonderland*. I was bored by it.

During the oil crisis of 1917, when Father had to keep in touch with his suppliers in Oklahoma, transactions sometimes took place in the evenings because of the time difference. Then Mother would take over the reading aloud and Father would wrestle with his enemy, the telephone. It stood on the windowsill on the stair landing, within easy earshot of the whole house. He would begin in a normal voice.

"Hello. Central." The receiver hook would be jiggled a trifle impatiently. "Central...hello, hello...Central? I want to talk to Tulsa, Oklahoma."

A pause.

In a louder tone, "I said TULSA, OKLAHOMA."

Pause.

Still louder, "TULSA, OKLAHOMA. T-U-L-S-A."

Pause. Then, impatiently, "Yes, I'll give you the number. And I want to talk person-to-person to Mr._____." At this point he probably had to spell the man's name.

At this point, also, Mother was beginning to fidget. Then, from the landing in a half-bellow, "HELLO, TULSA?

IS THAT YOU, HARRY? WAIT A MINUTE I CAN'T HEAR YOU."

Much jiggling of the receiver hook, followed by, "CENTRAL! CAN'T YOU CLEAR THIS LINE? I'M TALKING TO TULSA, OKLAHOMA."

Pause.

"NO! They did NOT hang up. You've cut us off!"

Then the whole process would start over again, the decibels rising as frustration mounted. Father would return in a lather; Mother would be in a tizzy; and I would be torn between my sympathy for Central and my embarrassment over Father's impatience; torn, probably, between Mother's standards of courtesy and Father's of efficiency.

If I was brash enough to beg for one more story after such a session, Father's angry, stormy face would break into a radiant smile and he would say, "Go 'long, you old fraud-on-the-government, you know it's beddyhouse time. Off you go—instanter!"

So I would drag myself up to my room pondering the strange ways of a father who could be so mean to Central and so loving with me.

I wish I had a glossary of his favorite words: "instanter," "beddyhouse," and such. He had a large and effective vocabulary which he had gleaned from his reading; but since it had been learned visually, he often mispronounced what his ear had not learned to hear. We loved it when Mother would tease him about his big words. She liked the brisk Anglo Saxon ones; he relished the sonority of the polysyllables.

"Why don't you just say 'please pass the jam' instead of 'I'd like some more of those strawberry conserves, please'?"

"But they are conserves," he would argue. "In my boyville when we brought in the berries to Mother, she didn't just make 'jam' out of them, she conserved them. The same with pickles and everything else. She had to conserve things if we wanted to eat."

So he went on saying "conserves" and/or "preserves"

and she went on saying "jam," and we had our choice.

Choice of words was one thing, but pronunciation was another. Here he was always humble. One early twist that even he laughed about was his attempt to quote the motto of the Order of the Garter. An avid reader of history and a great admirer of the British aristocracy, he was trying to tell Mother the romantic story of the origin of that motto, *Honi soit qui mal y pense*. What he came out with sounded like On a Sway Camollipop! I suspect the distortion had grown with every telling until by the time it reached me it was outrageous, but Father was not above making a good story better, even when the joke was on him.

ANN ARBOR INTERLUDE

IN THE FALL of 1916 we rented a house in Ann Arbor for a year. I always understood that we did so because Mother liked small town living, and Ann Arbor at that time had a population of only about 28,000, not counting the University. Many of Mother's close friends had already migrated there, some with children we already knew. Thus we young ones were transplanted into familiar soil. The difference was that Father was now a commuter. Weekends were his only real family times.

Our rented house was no beauty, but it had plenty of space around it and it housed us all comfortably enough. Architecturally it was Dutch colonial, if anything—white below and dark green above with a veranda across the front and dark oak woodwork inside. It stood on a large lot at the corner of Wayne and Washtenaw where the Christian Science Church is now. Washtenaw has become such a busy street that it is hard to remember it wasn't even paved when we lived there. The pavement stopped three blocks short of us at Oxford Road, and the now-vanished streetcar tracks turned westward just before that. We were on the edge of town where traffic was light. An occasional horse-drawn wagon lumbered by. I remember hitching a ride on the tail of one and being roundly scolded by Mother, but cars were so few that I actually learned to ride my first bicycle right there on Washtenaw Avenue.

The public school I went to that year was the old Tappan, housed in a dark red brick building which has since been superceded by more important buildings as the University campus has expanded. Tappan, named for a former president of the University, was pronounced in the old fashioned way with the accent on the second syllable. I entered its third grade with some trepidation. I loved my teacher, Miss Finer, but was terrified of our principal, Miss Cook. Miss Cook used to appear on the steps at

recess time and stand watching us with folded arms and
tightly closed lips, effectively dampening any exhuberance
on our part.

In third grade we were deemed old enough to have song
books. From them we learned to read music in solfeggio
and had to sing our songs in do-re-mi before we could put
the real words in. That was a great advance over learning
by ear and made us feel very grown up. On the other hand,
my art education died a-borning when they tried to teach
me to draw. An apple—a juiceless, cold thing—and a tulip
without color were my only accomplishments in that line.
But we had a good grounding in the multiplication tables
up to the twelves, and we learned to write sentences
properly.

One of my classmates was a little colored girl named
Portia Bethel. (We never called negroes "blacks." That
would have been derogatory. And we were never ever
allowed to use the word "nigger.") Portia lived right
behind us and her family kept chickens. The rooster's crow
at dawn is part of my memory of those Ann Arbor days. I
usually walked home with Portia. Quite often we were
accompanied by another classmate named Minty Waldron.
Minty, the son of our doctor, was an extremely
good-looking little boy. When teased about always
walking with us, his reply allegedly was, "Well, you have
to be nice to girls or when you grow up they won't marry
you." Minty needn't have worried. When he grew up he
married one of the most beautiful and fascinating of
women who was neither Portia Bethel nor I.

Margaret, down at the high school (the old Ann Arbor
High on the corner of Huron and State) had a full-fledged
crush on her Latin teacher, Jessie Mary Brown. Miss
Brown was known to a little circle of worshippers, of
which Marg was one, as J.M.B. The girls made up songs
about her, wrote poems to her, enjoyed her pungent wit
and cherished her rare kind words. They also learned
Latin. When the Latin Club put on its annual play, Marg
took Mother and Father to it. To her joy, J.M.B. stood at
the door of the auditorium, hand outstretched. Margaret
siezed it eagerly. "Miss Brown, these are my parents," she

said proudly. Miss Brown freed her hand without a word and held it out to Father. "Tickets, please," she said, unsmiling. Margaret was mortified; Mother convulsed.

We had a black couple working for us that year, Gussie and Willis. She was thin and sad and a superlative cook; he was happy-go-lucky and lazy. He thought it great fun to charge into a mob of students in our Studebaker with the "California top" and watch the boys scatter. He had nothing against students; he just liked fun and games.

Richard had contracted typhoid fever at camp the summer before our move and spent most of that fall in bed. In the winter, when he had recovered sufficiently, Mother and Father went to California for a vacation, leaving the four of us in the care of a practical nurse whose name I don't remember. Nor do I want to. She was known simply as "The Fat Lady."

She was indeed fat. When Willis had to hoist her into the car with a manly shove from behind, her cheerful "ups-a-daisy" sent us into paroxysms of giggles. She was very firm about what she considered to be our slovenly ways. We had to wash, not just polish, our shoes, and her ideas of neatness were much more stringent than ours. Louise, describing to Mother in far-off California the new regimen, said, "One thing she did for you right away was clean up your desk, Mother." That almost brought Mother home forthwith, but Father calmed her down. He didn't want his golf vacation spoiled. "The damage is already done, my dear," he pointed out. "As long as she keeps the children safe and healthy, what does it matter if she has read your private correspondence and knows what your bank balance is?"

When they returned, Mother promptly got rid of The Fat Lady. Only her echo stayed with us—her "ups-a-daisy."

With our parents home that spring, one of our pleasures became driving around the countryside on weekends. Father's farm upbringing had given him a good eye for fertile land and healthy crops, and his comments on the animals we saw, the way this farmer or that kept his fences, or his barns, began to stir my interest in things rural.

One fateful day, we turned in at the driveway of one of those farms. The barns didn't look like much, but the house was a substantial, sturdy-looking one, the grey granite blocks that formed its lower story shot through with soft pink and the second story showing some half timbering above the long front porch.

"Who lives here?" I wanted to know.

"Some people named Brokaw," Marg answered. "Look at all those cows. I wonder if they're friendly."

"But why are we stopping?" I persisted.

I never got an answer for we had arrived, and the introductions took all attention away from me. I was puzzled, because we seemed to be expected, and yet I had never heard of these people before. We were invited in, politely, so I trailed along with the rest, too shy to ask any more questions.

Inside the heavy front door, an oak stairway with two sharp turns in it rose from the hall to the mysterious second floor. On the right of the hall was a front parlor with drawn shades giving it a gloomy, almost spooky, look. I was allowed only a quick peek, for which I was thankful. Then we were ushered across the hall to the other front room, a chilly dining room. Both rooms had corner fireplaces faced with tiny, shiny tiles, mauve in the one room and pink in the other, and neither fireplace looked as though it had ever held a merry, warming fire. At the back, facing south towards the river, was a much more cheerful living room where I would have been glad to stay, but as that was where the adults chose to sit, I was turned over to the daughter of the house, a girl about my own age whose name was Eleanor. Eleanor and I went outside to play.

The outside was lovely. The lawn was just the kind I liked, with thick grass, not too often mowed, growing right up to the porch steps. There were several tall trees, an elm and a walnut and a hoary old fir, and a row of maples marking the lane that led back to the barns. Beyond the barns were a couple of meadows sloping down towards the river.

More than once we stopped at that farm. Eleanor
patiently showed me her side of the place -- the kittens in
the barns, which maple trees were the best for climbing --
but I never knew why we stopped until one day about
supper time. Father had just come home from Detroit. I
had not seen him yet when Marg came dancing into the
dining room, hugging herself and chanting, "We've bought
the Brokaw farm! WE'VE BOUGHT THE BROKAW
FARM! It's OURS! We're going to live there!" Whatever
Marg was enthusiastic about I knew must be wonderful, so
I joined in the general cheer at the news, but I had no idea
then of the change it was going to make in my life to live in
the country.

THE WAR YEARS

THAT CHANGE did not take place immediately. When America's entry into the Great War sent its shock waves through the country I was still pretty well protected from them within the fortress of our family unity. Father was too old for the army and Dick was too young. But Father was deeply involved in a vital war industry and this made it essential that we move back to Detroit for the duration.

Nevertheless, the farm had its influence upon me as I tried to adjust to it in those unsettling years. We used it as a weekend and vacation retreat. "Why can't I stay home?" I would whine as the family prepared on Friday for two days in the country. "I could sleep at Doris's. Her mother said so." But Mother who knew Doris's mother very well, was quite aware of who had dreamed that one up.

"No, dear. You're coming with us." And if my whining continued, Marg would probably come in with some enticing idea like, "You know there may be a new batch of kittens out in the barns. You'd better come." So, sulkily, I would go along. Then by Monday morning, I was often so entranced with farm life that I sulked all the way home in the car. But Virginia Park was still my true home and I was glad to be back at Miss Newman's School with Doris when fall came.

Home life was different now. After a long day at the office, Father would return tired, snatch up the evening paper and pour over the maps showing the changing battle lines. There was no time for reading aloud. When she could, Mother would gather us around the piano to sing together, but now the songs were different. Stephen Foster's melancholy ballads were replaced by "Keep the Home Fires Burning" or "There's a Long, Long Trail A-winding," or, in a more stirring vein, "Over There" or "The Caisson Song". We sang all four verses of "My Country 'Tis of Thee," but the third verse of "The Star Spangled Banner," the one in which Francis Scott Key

damned the British so eloquently, was quietly dropped.
Father's good strong bass and Mother's high soprano left
the inner parts to Margaret and Louise. I warbled along
with Mother and quickly learned all the words of both
verse and chorus of most songs, but I never learned to sing
alto.

Three of Father's seven sisters had sons of draft age,
and we were proud to have those handsome cousins join
our family circle whenever they were stationed near
enough to come for weekend leaves. Of the seven in
uniform, I remember three best, the two dashing and
handsome McCulloughs from Pennsylvania and another
handsome one, Laurin Hunter, from Duluth.

At the front end of our hall at 115 Virginia Park, next to
the den and opposite the green-carpeted stairway, a tiled
vestibule served as a mud room where we dropped our
roller skates in summer and our overshoes in winter. A
curtained, plate glass inner door shielded the hall from
drafts when the front door was opened. It was in that
vestibule that they hid the doll buggy which was my
Christmas present the year I was eight. It was 1917. That
Christmas morning, as usual we were up early. The
eleventh commandment in our house was that on
Christmas morning, breakfast came before presents. But
who can sleep until breakfast time on Christmas morning?
By the time it was light we four were waiting impatiently
in the den for Mother and Father to come down. The living
room, where the stockings were hung, of course was off
limits. Margaret was peering through the lace curtains at
the almost empty street when, behold! there came a lone
soldier, walking fast, his breath visible in the frosty air.

"Here comes a good looking one," she cried, drawing
Louise to her side. Then, "It's Laurin!" she shrieked, and led
a dash to open the front door for him. Dick stopped me at
the inner door.

"You can't come in here, Eliz," he said firmly, mindful of
the hidden doll buggy. "You wait in the hall." A tradition
was a law to conscientious Richard. So I must needs wait,
dancing up and down in my excitement until Laurin came
through and gave me a hug and a kiss just like the big girls.

I was ecstatic! I had been kissed by a soldier! I don't remember much about the doll buggy, but I do remember that Christmas.

It must have been a still earlier one, probably just pre-war, when another set of cousins came to visit. Aunt Mary Stephenson, Mother's sister from Duluth, was a gifted pianist and had made of her family a small orchestra. How they traveled with all their instruments, or where they stayed in our crowded house, I do not remember, but when they assembled in our living room, Elizabeth with her cello, Bill with his violin, Johnny at his traps, and Aunt Mary at our upright piano, they made wonderful music. Uncle Jack, with a fine ear but no training, contributed a lilting obligato on a little tin whistle. I loved the tin whistle! On that Christmas morning in the midst of all the confusion of shredded tissue paper and discarded ribbons, of exclamations of delight or surprise and of thanks inadequately expressed, Uncle Jack's quick ear caught the strains of a German band serenading us. Those roving brass bands were a Christmas tradition in Detroit before the anti-German mania of the war swept them into oblivion. Uncle Jack, sympathizing with their cold and thankless lot, called them in to warm themselves by our fire. In gratitude they gave us their whole repertoire of German carols, played at full ear-splitting volume.

One reason for our custom of delaying the opening of presents until after breakfast was so Mother's brother, Uncle Alec Beal, could get there in time to share the fun with us. Uncle Alec, whose disastrous first marriage had left him childless, was slow-spoken, with a twinkle in his eye and a round bald head. He smoked loathsome cigars, gave us wet kisses and wonderful presents and used such words as "yup" and "nope" to our delight and Mother's distress. The year my sisters and brother were old enough to have wrist watches, I was far too young. As a joke, I got a toy one in the toe of my stocking. Alas, my sense of humor did not stretch quite that far and I must have made my disappointment all too obvious. The next Christmas, Uncle Alec gave me a fine gold wrist watch. What's more, he made Mother promise to let me wear it. Dear Uncle Alec!

Traditions like those Christmas ones continued to hold us together, but changes, both external and internal to the family, were beginning to affect our close little circle. As a girl, Mother's ambition had been to go to Vassar, but her father would not let her go without her older sister, Mary. Aunt Mary adamantly refused to take four years of Latin, and Vassar adamantly refused to consider anyone who didn't. Therefore, Mother couldn't go. Therefore, her daughters must go! But to get there we had to pass the dread College Entrance Examinations of the New York State Board of Regents. These were tough, especially for girls from public high schools. The best access was through an eastern preparatory school whose faculty were specialists in cramming the right information into young minds. Margaret's variegated academic career, three different high schools in three years, had not prepared her for those rigorous College Boards, at least so thought Mother and Father. So Margaret was packed off to Dwight School in Englewood, New Jersey, for her last high school year. And because it had always been assumed that what was good for Margaret was good for Louise, Louise went, too. It meant two years of torment for Louise who never got over her homesickness, but both girls made the grade. Margaret was admitted with two "conditions" and probably would not have got in at all if Father had not gone down personally and, as he said, helped her over the brick wall of the dean's resistance. Louise sailed in unaided.

Meanwhile, in 1918, with the war still going on, a rumor got about that the draft age might be lowered to 16. Dick, at age 14, had never been away from home except for that disastrous summer at camp when he got typhoid fever, and our parents decided he would be able to cope better with army life, should he be called up, if he had some experience with non-parental discipline first. He was sent off to Choate School, in Wallingford, Connecticut, there to be taught, along with the usual college preparatory courses, close order drill. But—oh, ignominy!—they had to use wooden rifles. There were no real ones to be spared for "little boys."

"The wooden rifles were bad enough," said Dick many years later, "but they weren't the worst of it. My heroes," he continued, "weren't the kind who marched in the ranks. My heroes stalked the Red Man silently and alone. They overcame the enemy single-handedly by superior cunning and courage." Fortunately, Heroic Richard did not have to endure the shame of the wooden rifles very long, for the war ended soon. He finished his high school years at Choate and then came back to the University of Michigan.

With all three of my siblings suddenly removed from the family circle, home life was different. My school day ran from 8:00 in the morning to 1:00 p.m. Then I walked or skated the six blocks home for lunch with Mother. Whatever Mother's involvement with war work or civic uplift, she was always waiting for me when I got home from school.

"I'm starved!" was my first cry as I came in the door. "What's for lunch?"

I had two favorite menus that would send me flying to get my hands washed and hair brushed so we could sit down and get through with grace quickly. One was sardines and cheese toast with tomatoes on the side; the other was salmon loaf with hard boiled egg sauce. While I stuffed myself, Mother would listen sympathetically to my tales of woe about the teacher who didn't understand me or, rarely, to my boasting about a good mark on a test. Once I remember telling her about the girl who had smashed her beautiful Christmas doll when she found out it was made in Germany. Mother was as shocked as I was. To me it was infanticide; to her it was the kind of fanaticism which her whole nature deplored. I was much closer to Mother that year than when the others were around.

On the seventh of November, four days before the war ended officially, I was playing outside when all at once factory whistles started blowing, church bells burst into joyous clangor, drivers honked their horns and people on the street stopped to look at each other with a wild surmise. I ran to Mother.

"What's happening?" I asked.

She came running down the stairs from the telephone.

"The war is over!" she cried. "Come on—quickly! We must go!"

She swept me into the back seat of the car with her and said to the driver, "Take us downtown!"

"Where to, Mrs. Earhart?" he asked.

"It doesn't matter! Just go to the center! Go toward the river."

I had never seen her a-glow like that.

We had to go at a crawl because of the chaotic traffic. There were no traffic lights or stop signs at the cross streets. Model T's mingled with Studebakers, Franklins, and Packards in joyous confusion. Horns honked incessantly, but in friendly salute, not impatience. At every intersection more and more cars, some of other forgotten makes, joined our procession as we edged our way toward the river. We came to a standstill finally at the Campus Martius, the great open hub of the city, now called Kennedy Square, where the old City Hall faced its matching County Building across acres of park. The Square was thronged with people—dancing, cheering, waving, chanting people, young and old. Flags were everywhere; horns blew; perfect strangers would embrace, laughing, and push on to embrace the next one. We could not get out of the car so close was the press of the crowd around us, but Mother drank it all in. It was a deeply emotional moment for her. A Detroiter born, she had seen her pleasant hometown grow into the fourth largest city in the country. Now the weapons and machines it had produced had won the greatest war in history. Detroit was mad with joy and pride. That pulsing mass of people was the very heart of the city—her city—and it was a heart beating high.

PART III

1920 - 1930

CULTURE SHOCKS

THE TWENTIES "roared" in as the tides of war receded into history. During the teens when the country was at war, I had been at peace, for our family remained intact. But during the twenties when the country was at peace, I was at war—at war with my parents and at war within myself. We children were caught between the rock of our parents' Victorian beliefs about right and wrong and the seething whirlpool of our own generation's search for new meanings in a chaotic world.

It was the age of the flapper. Women had lost much of their femininity. Skirts were short and skimpy; corsets disappeared along with the hourglass figure; chests were flat; waistlines descended to the hips; stockings were rolled below the knees. We called our big winter overshoes "artics." (Only sissies said "arctics.") Their closure flaps had buckles which every teenager knew better than to fasten, and it was the flapping of those black wings about our ankles that gave rise to the word "flapper."

The sporting male appeared on the golf course in loose, baggy knickers called "plus-fours," with knee-length argyle socks to match his pullover sweater. He wore his hair parted in the middle and pasted down with "bear's grease" to give his head the patent leather look affected by film star, Rudolph Valentino. The name of Valentino's most famous character, the Sheik, soon became a common noun and was applied to any young man whose good looks and seductive ways could charm the female heart. (The book, which was much more explicit than the film, we girls read inside our text books during study hall.)

For women, the pompadour and those puffs over the ears which were stuffed with "rats" to make them stand out, gave way to the boyish bob or the permanent wave. Margaret, who as usual was our leader in breaking new ground, secretly saved her money and when she had $20 went without a word to anyone and got a permanent. She came home with her hair bobbed and in a glorious frizz to face Mother's, "Oh, Margie! How could you?"

Dress for evening was quite formal. When dining out, even at each other's homes, tuxedos or "white-tie-and-tails" were appropriate for men any time after six o'clock, and the women wore knee-length, shimmery, backless dresses with lots of beads, sequins, and/or fringe. Father looked with heavy disapproval upon the immoderate display of female flesh those styles called for, and with pride on Mother's taste for chiffon and lace. The two of them were at dinner with friends one night at the Detroit Athletic Club, dressed according to their standards of decorum, when for some reason one of the ladies in their party came to the table late. The gentlemen, of course, rose with alacrity. Unfortunately, Father's chair intercepted a waiter who was just bringing a plate of oysters on the half shell to a modishly dressed lady at the table behind him. Oysters and ice all cascaded down her bare back. The lady shrieked; the waiter fled; the head waiter found an urgent need to be elsewhere. Father alone had to wipe up the naked back, chivalry and modesty in raging conflict within him.

Clara Bow, the girl who had "It," was Hollywood's sex symbol. The movie industry's appointed arbiter of good taste, known as the Hays Office, limited the amount of exposure allowed to Clara's physical charms, as it limited the number of seconds a kiss could last on film, but Clara got her message across anyway. Sex had moved out of the bedroom and into the rumble seat. Or onto the park bench. Or to any other convenient place, public or private. Sex was no longer a sacred expression of spiritual love. It was a game to be played, blatantly, boastfully, with a score to be kept and bragged about. This profaning of what, to them, was a truly sacred rite, was highly distressing to our parents. Their disgust with the cheapening of sex became a major factor in our confusion. Open expressions of affection between us girls and our female friends Mother smiled upon, but let a boy come too close and all the weight of hell and damnation came between us! As Marg said, some years later, "If Mother had been half as relaxed about our heterosexual friendships as she was about our homosexual ones, it would have made courtship much easier."

The XVIII Amendment, passed and ratified while a large part of the male population was away at war, brought no change in our habits at home. One rock from which Mother would not budge was her abhorrance of liquor. She had seen the effect of alcoholism in her own family as a girl and had highly charged emotions about alcohol in any form. She told me once, "Oh, Elizabeth, if I thought liquor had ever passed your lips, I would be broken hearted!" Therefore it was with a certain glee that we witnessed her discomfiture shortly before we left Detroit. Unknown to us, David Wallace & Sons, the grocers with whom she had done business for years, had once sent her a bottle of whiskey as a Christmas present. Mother, not knowing how to refuse it, had hidden it away at the back of her closet where the maids wouldn't find it. "It might be needed some day for medicinal purposes," she apologized to Father. There it remained even after Prohibition became the law of the land.

Then came a day when she was chatting on the telephone by the big back window on the landing and watching a house being built in the block behind us. To her horror, she saw a workman fall from the roof. She broke off her conversation, ran for the "medicinal" bottle and rushed across the alley to the scene of the disaster. The man was not seriously hurt, but an ambulance had been summoned. The foreman gave the fallen man one swig from the bottle, then returned it to Mother with a conspiratorial wink and said, "Better get it out of sight, Lady. The police will be here soon." Mother slunk home in chagrin, her secret revealed and her motive misconstrued. She re-hid the bottle in a dark corner of the topmost shelf in the butler's pantry. There it stayed until our cook's husband found it. When it became evident that he was enjoying it on the sly, he was promptly fired and, alas, his wife went with him. The remaining contents of the bottle went down the drain.

Poor Mother! She was like the little Dutch boy who stuck his finger in the leaking dike to hold back the ocean. Detroit was located ideally for illicit "rum running." America had boasted for years of its long unguarded border with Canada. At Detroit that border was formed by waters anyone with a speed boat could cross undetected. And cross it they did, professional bootleggers and private citizens alike, anyone who did not choose to obey the law. In fact, breaking the law—the XVIII Amendment in particular—became just another game to be snickered about. Mother was appalled by this attitude on the moral ground that all drinking was evil; Father was appalled by the breakdown in respect for the Constitution. But on all sides, we young ones heard the snickers.

During those years when such conflicts were challenging the mores of families like ours, Marg was my anchor. It was Marg to whom I turned for understanding and interpretation. She never squelched my questionings even when her answer was, "I don't know." However, in 1920 when we moved to the farm, she and Louise and Dick were all away at school. Suddenly, at age twelve, I found myself an only child in a wholly new environment and I had many things to figure out for myself.

My first two friends in the country were neighbors. One was Eleanor Brokaw from whose father we had bought the farm. He, in turn, had bought the farm just west of us. The other was Bessie Parker whose father owned the grist mill at the corner of Dixboro Road. We three girls swam in the Parker millpond, slithered our way through the moss-grown spill to wade downstream toward the Huron River. There was one spot where the mire was hip deep and we could sink into that delicious, cool, slippery, clinging mud until our bare feet struck bottom. What would have happened it there had been no bottom, never troubled us. Just Mother. With Eleanor I explored our barns where she had played in her time, jumped in the hay, and discovered the new batches of kittens that were born to the barn cats that were her friends. At milking time, we were given milk still warm from the cow. All these joys Eleanor and Bessie initiated me into with patience and probably amusement.

Bessie went to the one-room school that was halfway between her house and mine. Many a PTA function I attended there as I tagged along with her and her other friends to the evening affairs. Eleanor showed me one Saturday how to climb through a window with a broken catch. With no one around, the place became our secret playroom.

It was mostly in the summer, though, that I played with those girls. When school began in September, I went to town driven by our large, stupid, good natured Stanley whose job was dignified by the name *chauffeur*. I was so embarrassed over having a *chauffeur* that I made Stanley let me out two blocks from school so I could arrive on foot like everyone else.

In the absence of his older children, Father did his best to keep in touch with me and my friends. He organized nutting parties on fall weekends when we would scour the fence rows where the walnut, hickory and butternut trees grew, each of us with a gunny sack for her findings. We would bring our trophies back to spread them out in the basement to season, our hands black with the stain from the walnut husks, our blood tingling from the crisp air, and our appetites whetted for the cider and doughnuts we were offered. In the winter, when the outer husks had all been shucked and the nuts dried, there would always be a bowl of them on the dinner table after dessert. Father would crack them with a hammer, and he, Mother, and I would sit companionably picking out the kernels while he recalled stories of his "boyville" or recounted to Mother the events of his day in Detroit. Those after-dinner sessions were very peaceable—too peaceable, actually, for real communication, for I was adept at tuning out all that did not concern me directly.

Soon I found that living three miles out of town had its good points as well as its bad. Though I missed the easy companionship of walking home with the other girls or dropping in at will at their houses, our farm held all sorts of allure for those town girls. Our house had plenty of room for slumber parties, and Mother and Father were always cordial. My new friends took delight in the mysteries of cow barns, hay mows and pig sties, and thanks to what I had learned from Eleanor and Bessie, I was now the expert. I became the leader! This was heady stuff.

At a certain houseparty that brought me a bit of notoriety on the underground circuit, I exercised this leadership in a way that, fortunately, never came to the attention of my parents. I had five or six friends for a slumber party that weekend. As with all such gatherings, slumber was not our first interest. The sleeping porch to which we were consigned was a safe distance from my parents' room, and when they, trusting souls, had gone to sleep, I led my crew in their night clothes down the road to the empty schoolhouse. It was no trick at all to climb in through the window with the broken catch. The full moon gave us plenty of light; the two little reed organs gave us plenty of noise; and the empty blackboard gave scope to such wit and such art as our giggles allowed us to commit to it. We must have played there for a couple of hours. Then, carefully cleaning the blackboard and obliterating any other signs we could see of our illicit fun, we made our way back to bed, and this time to slumber.

While I was learning about country life in Michigan, Margaret was off learning about life on the Labrador coast. It was customary at Vassar for juniors to take a summer job out in the world, doing good or earning money, whichever suited their circumstances. Mother's strong interest in missionary work found an echo in Marg's interest in social service. She applied to Sir Wilfred Grenfell to go with his Medical Mission to Labrador in the summer of 1922. Her letters told of all sorts of adventures. I, for one, was both horrified and thrilled to learn that she had had to assist at the birth of a child born unexpectedly early. Birth was a sacred event! Only doctors and angels were present at a birth! What went on when a baby was born, anyway?

That was the kind of knowledge we were protected from. The very word "sex" was scarcely uttered above a whisper. Yet if there is any place where birth is not a mystical concept, it is on a dairy farm. Unfortunately, I was so far behind the brood of our farm manager's children in my knowledge of the sex life of cows that I dared not show my ignorance by asking them questions. I came at the matter obliquely through Father who, I knew, applauded rather than scoffed at ignorance about sex.

"What's the difference between a heifer and a cow?" I asked him one day as we waked towards the barns. The smell of the barnyard rose all around us, redolent of things primordial and earthy. But Father's answer showed that his mind was on a higher plane.

"God, in his infinite wisdom," he said, "gives a cow the wonderful ability to produce milk only when she has brought a new life into the world. Until she gives milk, she is a heifer."

"Oh," I said. I dared no more.

Bulls were not mentioned. There was so much that was not mentioned! It was a long time before I found out the difference between a bull and a steer.

HIGH SCHOOL

IN THE EARLY '20s we did not have junior high schools. At that time, the old Ann Arbor High School was uncrowded enough that its lower floor was given over to what they called "Central Eighth Grade." We eighth graders were lowliest of the low, in every sense. If we ventured upstairs, as we rarely did, we were looked upon as mere bothersome children by those superior beings who lived above us.

It was not a good year for me academically, that Central Eighth Grade, but two important things happened to me which had a far deeper effect on my life than getting a D in beginning Latin. My parents took me with them when they went to North Carolina for their winter vacation, and there I learned to ride horseback! This was bliss! This was IT! It was freedom and power and the joy of pure action, and it put no strain at all on my lazy brain. The homework I had brought along to study lay unregarded in my room while I dreamed great dreams of the glorious exploits I would someday perform on my own magnificent thoroughbred before cheering multitudes. What price Latin then? When Marg joined us for her spring break, supposedly to tutor me, not even her magic touch could keep my mind on Latin. I had fallen in love with horses!

The other event of importance came after I got home. I acquired a Best Friend. For this country girl who had played alone so much, it was a new experience. Her name, like mine, was Elizabeth, but we all called her Bud. She was an incurable romantic with a bright inquiring mind, an insatiable interest in people, and the most infectious laugh in the world. Like me, she was crazy about horses. In fact, we were crazy about most kinds of animals except boys. We would have been interested in boys if they had been interested in us, but we were two late bloomers and found greater pleasure in four-legged animals and other growing things. To be sure, growing things included our more advanced girl friends, but our interest in their love life was vicarious. Our joy was to explore the countryside on horseback.

When we had first bought the farm from the Brokaws back in 1917, the old barns were in deplorable state and were much too near the house for Mother's fastidious nose. Father had had them torn down and had built beautiful big new ones across the road and at the corner of what came to be called Earhart Road. Here the Holstein herd, which was his pride, stood patiently with their heads in stanchions at milking time. Two round silos held the ensilage that fed them through the winter, and the hay mows over the stables held food for the great farm horses.

After my foray to North Carolina with my parents, Father added a pair of riding horses to the livestock. Bud and I loved nothing better than to brush and curry our pets, saddle them up ourselves, and take off up the hill. The road veered slightly around a spreading oak tree that had probably been there before the white man came. At the top of the hill was the little cemetery where the earliest settlers of Washtenaw County were buried. A little farther on, we would come to the forty-acre wood lot where Father had had some trails cut through the underbrush. Here we could meander as we pleased, confident that no matter how lost we got, the horses would know the way back to the barn. In the spring the woods were golden with the daffodils Mother had had planted there to grow wild among the native violets and spring beauties, the hepaticas and bloodroot. In the fall, when the maples put on their glorious pageant of color, and even in the winter, with the trees bending under a weight of snow or with each twig sheathed in ice and the bushes below looking like fairy castles, we loved the woods. And if our horses pranced a bit in the crisp air, we loved that, too. Were we not masters of the powerful creatures?

In the privacy of that forty-acre domain, we discussed

weighty matters like: to smoke or not to smoke; to neck or not to neck; who was dating whom; or what did *she* see in *him?* Snatches of our conversation come back to me now and then.

"Do you think Fran necks with every date she goes out with?" I ask naively.

"You bet she does," says my wise friend. "How do you think she gets so many dates?"

"Oh, dear!" I exclaim, shocked. "And Mother keeps telling me what a lovely girl she is! Well, I won't tell Mother. No sense in disillusioning her."

This instinct to protect our parents from Reality was probably only a reflection of their attempts to protect our innocence, but we didn't recognize it as such. We only knew that we knew more about life than they did, and we must not tell them our secrets.

We did not spend all our time on horseback, though. Bud, whose heart took in the whole world, had friends in every group, no matter how closed their little circles seemed to be, and where she went she drew me with her. I joined the Girl Reserves, a small and solemn group of do-gooders, the Colony Club, a large club of girls with a vague purpose I have forgotten, and miraculously I was invited to be in The Shakespearean Circle, a very select group of upper classmen who met in our different homes to put on one act plays. I made other friends, too, in more casual ways. So gradually, under Bud's unconscious leadership, I became a social creature instead of the loner I had been. As my friendships widened, self-confidence increased and my grades came up. I was even able to pass Cicero with an A at the end of my junior year.

Richard had been absorbed into campus and fraternity life by this time and did not eat at home often. Margaret and Louise were away at Vassar. This left me alone to interpret the world—the young world, the new world, my world—to Mother and Father. Dinner table conversations grew less peaceable. My parents were vocal in deploring the awful things that were in store for the country if the churches continued to lose the young people. At those sessions I was the sole defender of the generation that had been labelled "flaming youth." After listening to one of Mother's outbursts about the evils of sex, drink, and irreligion, none of which practices were real issues between me and my friends yet, I stormed out of the dining room in tears.

"You think we're all like that, you and your friends! Well, we're NOT! We don't all drink! We don't all smoke! And we have our own religion even if we don't like church!" With that crushing manifesto I fled to my room and slammed the door.

Father went riding with me the next day, a custom that had superceded the nutting parties of yore.

"So your friends have their own religion, but they don't like church, is that it?" he began, keeping his horse level with mine. Our country roads were still gravel and free enough of traffic that we could ride side by side.

"Well," I countered defensively, "you don't like the church either. You're always complaining about the way it's run."

"Touché," he laughed, "but that's only the business side of it. Some of those good people have no idea in the world how to run a business. But I don't fault their religion."

"But they're so..." I couldn't think of the right word. "They're so stuffy...they're so organized about it! Why does it have to be organized, anyway?"

"My dear child," said my parent, growing pontifical, "with the world in the state it's in, don't you think this is the very time we need organized religion?"

When he got going on the state of the world, I recognized defeat. He knew so much more than I did about the adult world and could quote his authorities, while my only authorities were my young friends and our half-formed ideas. I kicked my horse into a gallop, sending a shower of gravel into Father's face. By the time he caught up with me he was chortling.

"Well, that's one way to win an argument," he said.

* * *

When Margaret and Louise came home for vacations, the dinner table conversations sometimes grew even livelier. Joyous as the reunions were, and full of laughter, we were no longer the closed circle we used to be. Louise was majoring in psychology with a strong interest in economics; Marg in English literature. These were fields about which Father felt life and his wide reading had taught him quite a bit, but it hadn't taught him the same things Vassar was teaching his beloved daughters.

"When I consider the vast sums I'm spending on your education," he used to thunder jokingly, "and you come home with hare-brained ideas like that!..."

Louise could let this run off her back, ("Poor Father, he's so used to being the boss, he doesn't like to be challenged."). But to Marg they were fighting words. ("Does he think I have to agree with him just because he's paying for my education?"). She tried to meet his challenges intellectually but her light rapier wit was no match for his heavy sabre thrusts and to avoid defeat she often took refuge in banter. This she did with great skill for she was a master of the light touch.

I would usually bear the brunt of her frustration and anger the next day as we rode together. "He's so dogmatic!" she would fume. "He quotes old fuddy-duddy Adam Smith and his 'enlightened self-interest' as though it were Holy Writ! What's so 'enlightened' about dog-eat-dog? I hate competition."

"Oh, come on, Marg! You don't mean that. You love football games."

"No, I don't. They're barbarous."

"I notice you go to them whenever you're asked."

"Yes, I know I do. But it's the crowds I like—and the color—and the people I see, not the game. I don't watch the game. I feel too sorry for the team that loses."

I could see her point about pity for the underdog, but I

knew Father would demolish that argument with scorn, and Marg did not like Father's scorn.

Mother said to me once, "Margie never quite dares to face an uncomfortable issue. You know how she is in a car, when you come to a cross street and she is afraid the driver on that street isn't going to stop? She ducks her head so as not to see the crash. That's just what she does with your father—she ducks her head."

So the tensions went on building between them, the bonds of similarity of character and of deep affection too strong for a rupture yet, but Marg turned more and more to a circle of friends who seemed to bolster her determination to find an identity for herself that was not tied to Father.

I sailed serenely along through sophomore and junior years in high school while Marg coped with her inner problems. She went through several beaux at that time, most of whom were looked upon with great disfavor by Mother. Some of them I loved. They used to take me along on their dates with Marg! Since the only beau of my own who paid me any attention was a boy I didn't like very well, such date-sharing was fine with me!

After graduation, Marg had first taken a job with E. P. Dutton & Company in New York City, writing blurbs for the books they published. That job didn't last long. When she came home, she first thought of teaching at Ann Arbor High, but as far as I know never got up her nerve to submit an application. Instead she went to work for the *Ann Arbor News* (I think it was the *Times News* then). She was determined to be independent of Father financially if she could. With the help of some wise and devoted friends, she struggled on with her identity crisis.

Then along came Clem Smith. Here was someone both Mother and Father could approve of! His father was Shirley W. Smith, Secretary of the University; his mother was one of the best-loved people in Ann Arbor. Both were devoted to Marg. Clem was one of that magic circle of friends whose intellectual interests as well as their understanding of complex family relationships bound them together. They all admired Marg. When Clem finally convinced her that marriage was a way to freedom rather than to "slavery," she and Clem became engaged. They were married on February 6, 1926.

Meanwhile, Louise had found her escape by a similar route. Her big adventure after junior year had been to go to Alaska to work at the Presbyterian Mission School at Haines with her roommate, Grace Hayward. Grace was very beautiful, as was Louise. Both had carried the daisy chain at Commencement when they were sophomores, a form of Beauty Contest that was peculiar to Vassar. Grace had many beaux, among them a theological student named Thornton Penfield. Thornton had a friend named Philip Guiles, also an aspiring theologian. The two young men were going to Alaska for the Presbyterian Missions to work their way up the coast in a small boat, stopping at native villages along the way and preaching as opportunity offered. Thornton had a violin; Phil an accordian. They would land with a first aid kit, use their music to gather a crowd, administer what first aid they could, if needed, and preach the gospel.

Thornton knew of the Mission School at Haines and of its need for extra help, so it was he who recruited the two Vassar girls to go there for the summer of 1923. Of course, when the young men landed their mission craft at Haines, they invited the girls to have dinner with them on the boat. Permission had to be sought from the matron, but Grace took care of that.

"They're old friends," she said, with slight accent on the old. "I've known them for ages. So have my parents."

With this reassurance, the girls were allowed to go unchaperoned to have dinner afloat. It was a welcome break in routine for all four of the young people, and they had a wonderful time. So wonderful that they forgot completely about the tide. The tides at Haines drop at least six feet. By the time the two cinderellas realized they should be back at the Mission, the dock was far above their heads. The two hosts had to hoist their fair guests up with more strength than dignity, and the girls fled, giggling, to get home in time to escape censure.

After that came other outings whenever the young men showed up at the Haines Mission, and if they seemed to show up more frequently as the summer wore on, it was not entirely by coincidence.

When Louise came home at the end of the summer, she was in love. She and I shared the sleeping porch which had been a kind of dormitory for us three sisters when Marg was there. But Marg was away that fall, so Louise and I had the porch to ourselves. As I lay sleepily in bed one morning in early September, dimly I heard Mother come in to waken us. She sat down on Louise's bed.

"Well, Weezy," she said gently, "so you're going to be a senior. Are you looking forward to it, dearie?"

Louise answered with a murmur which hardly penetrated my stupor, and the voices purred along. Then I heard Mother say, "Have you asked anyone to Senior Prom yet?"

"I know who I want to ask," I heard my sister say, "but I don't know whether he'll come."

"Oh?" said Mother, instantly alert. "Is it anyone I know?" she asked archly. (By this time I was becoming interested myself.)

"No," said Louise.

"How did you meet him, dear?" We both knew from bitter experience that Mother's standards demanded proper introductions.

"Oh, he and a friend of Grace's were working for the Presbyterians this summer. They're both theological students and we were the only white girls around so the four of us did things together."

"I see," said Mother, mollified by the sound church connection. "But what makes you think he might not come?"

"I don't know whether he could get away, or even if he'd want to go to a prom. He's older than all my friends. He might think we were too young for him."

"Mercy! How old is he?"

"He's almost thirty."

"Oh, nonsense, you goose! Of course he'll want to come if you ask him."

In due course, Louise did ask him. And he came. But there was a slight hitch! Because of his serious commitment to his career as a minister, Phil had given only a tentative acceptance. Of course he would love to come, his note said, but he wasn't sure of his time. He'd have to let her know later. Well, Grace was chairman of the prom, and Louise was on her committee. It was essential that Louise have a date. When no word came from Phil, finally, in desperation, they arranged with the brother of another friend to accept a last-minute invitation. Then word came from Phil that he would come! A message was hastily sent to the poor brother-of-a-friend, cancelling the second-class invitation.

The night of the prom, the girls waited nervously in their room for word to be brought that their dates had arrived.

"Miss Earhart," said the maid's voice at the door, "your young gentleman is downstairs."

Louise went happily down to greet Phil—only it wasn't Phil! It was the young-brother-of-a-friend. Then followed a mad scramble to find a last-minute date for him, for of course he couldn't be turned away in his elegant white tie and tails. The prom went on. Phil was there for the Grand March but had to leave soon after it. So began their year and a half of courtship.

DIVERGING ROADS

ON JUNE 3RD, 1925, Louise and Phil were married. It was a garden wedding, with a string trio, half hidden among the Persian lilacs, playing the wedding march. Tall baskets of peonies strung together with white ribbons formed an aisle that led to an improvised altar between two maple trees. Marg was maid of honor, two Vassar friends of Louise's, Grace Hayward and Florence Blackwell (better known as "Floppy"), were the bridesmaids. The bride was beautiful. Her dress, in the fashion of the day, was rather shapeless and came only to mid-calf, but a long veil of rose point lace gave it elegance. There was a hot wind blowing that day. It kept overturning the baskets of peonies, which rather diverted the guests, but I doubt if Louise even noticed it. Her eyes were upon the handsome young man who waited for her at the altar.

That wedding was the first permanent break in the family circle.

In the fall I was packed off to boarding school like my sisters before me. Reluctantly I went to Dana Hall in Wellesley, Massachusetts. It was probably the most miserable year of my life. My parents were right that dear old Ann Arbor High had not prepared me academically for the College Board examinations, but I loved Ann Arbor High and I wanted no part of New England. Dana Hall made it very clear to me that anything west of of the Hudson was considered inferior to anything in Massachusetts! For two summers I had enjoyed the freedom of camping in the Rockies with a group of other horse-loving girls. For six glorious weeks each summer we had explored the back country of Yellowstone Park on horseback, and the as-yet untrammeled Jackson Hole area. I was enamored of all things "Western." I was sure every cowboy I saw was a re-incarnation of my hero "The

Virginian." After the freedom and romance of those summers, the regimentation and the snobbery of an eastern boarding school were hard to take. My grades plummeted. So did my self-confidence. I wallowed in self-pity.

Added to my woes was a certain unease about Father. I knew he had had a mastoid operation in 1925, a very serious one in those days before antibiotics. When he had escorted Louise to the altar back in June, his head was still bandaged. What I did not know was that after I left for Dana Hall he underwent more operations for other ailments which were never explained to me.

I got a special dispensation and went home to be in Marg's wedding in February, but no one had time then to tell me what was wrong with Father. Perhaps the male urinary tract was considered too delicate a subject for my young ears. Father did not get to that wedding at all. He was upstairs in bed in the house on Arden Park in Detroit, which he and Mother had rented that winter. The ceremony took place downstairs, and was very quiet in deference to his illness. I, dressed in a short blue chiffon dress with beautiful slippers dyed to match it, but feeling very gauche in spite of them, was Marg's sole attendant. Marg was a-quiver with emotion as she came forward, alone, to meet Clem. I could see her bridal bouquet shake as she handed it to me. There was no hesitation in her mind about joining her life to Clem's, but strong feminist that she was, she didn't want to be called Mrs. Clement Andrew Smith. Furthermore, she didn't approve of religious rituals, but had to go through this one for Mother's sake. She was all for marriage, but not for weddings. Her own was a big compromise for her. For a time, she refused to wear her wedding ring, that symbol of slavery! However, when she lost it down a crack in the floor of the house they were building, she carefully marked the spot, eventually retrieved the ring, and as far as I know, wore it happily ever after.

I subsequently learned that, all told, Father had five

major operations in that year '25/'26, two of them probably unnecessary. He spent most of those months either in Harper or Ford Hospital in Detroit, or at the Mayo Clinic in Rochester, Minnesota. None of this came through to me in far off Dana Hall except in oblique references in the letters from home, and to be thus excluded only underscored my feelings of rejection.

Dick, in his senior year at Michigan, was closer to the situation. Much later he told me, "Father was hard on Mother in that period. He was impatient with her way of trying to help her church. She had signed a note in behalf of the church's building fund, which she did without consulting him and he scolded her for it. There were other things she had to handle alone, too, and he was critical of the way she did. He was a very sick man."

As a result of one of his operations he gave up sharing their big double bed, and moved into a separate room. There was a new relationship between them from then on, one which had its effect on me, though I was not aware of it right away.

Marg and Clem lived in Ann Arbor after their marriage, but their interests continued to diverge from ours. Clem taught rhetoric at the university for a year, then went through the University Medical School. As a pediatrician, he taught at the Harvard Medical School, became Chief of Staff at the Children's Hospital, and ultimately made a distinguished name for himself in the medical world as the father of Neo-natal Medicine. The chair in that discipline at the Harvard Medical School is named for him. Meanwhile Marg became active in social work, went on to get a Masters in it some years later, and tried her hand at writing for publication. Unfortunately, the manuscript of her book about the Brontës has been lost. Her accomplishments deserve a whole separate chronicle. I hope one of her daughters will write it someday.

Louise and Phil were held in the East, first by Phil's church work, then by his teaching at Andover-Newton Theological Seminary. In 1927 they went to Edinborough with their first-born child, Gwyneth, where Phil completed his Ph.D. in psychology. Back at Andover-Newton he became the mainspring in the movement to require clinical training for students planning to go into the ministry. As for Louise, for eight years she was on the Board of Commissioners for Foreign Missions of the Congregational Church, as well as studying violin and being active in musical circles.

Dick, after graduating in mechanical engineering from the University of Michigan had the hard choice to make between going on with engineering at which he was very good (he had been elected to Tau Beta Pi, the Engineering Honor Society) or casting his lot with Father. He chose the latter. He was sent to Wood River, Illinois, to the White Star refinery there, to learn about the oil business from that side firsthand, then came back to the main office in Detroit and devoted his time to the management end.

I passed my College Boards after that interminable year at Dana and finally got into Vassar. Though college life gave me great freedom compared to Dana Hall, I still yearned for things western, and to many of my new friends, Ann Arbor, Michigan, was "way out West!" The Dean felt this way, too, apparently, for when I applied to take my "Junior Year Abroad" at the University of Michigan, she informed me that going abroad junior year was for the purpose of seeking *culture*. Fortunately, I had support from the head of my department (I was a music major) who said, "Oh, yes, the University of Michigan has an excellent Music School. It should be a stimulating experience for you." I had my way for a year, but went back to Vassar to graduate with my class as Mother wanted me to do.

When Father regained his health and was back in charge of business affairs, his active mind turned to the future. With his long experience at riding the economic waves, he read the warnings in the behavior of the stock market. "We're riding for a fall," he prophesied as the '20s wore on, and he made his preparations accordingly. As early as

August of 1923 he had created trusts for Mother and for us
four children. These were to be our anchor to windward,
to keep us from ever "becoming a public charge," a
condition of shame in Father's mind. But more than that,
the management of our own incomes was to be training
for us in the fine art of stewardship. In a later letter to all
of us he expressed his philosophy this way:

> Under my philosophy of life, it seems to me an
> individual who is entrusted with more physical
> wealth than is required for [his] personal needs,
> becomes a trustee for the surplus, and that this
> surplus should be administered for the benefit
> of [his] fellow man and for posterity.

At first he managed the investments; we managed our
separate incomes.

In September of 1929, a month before "Black Monday"
brought on the Great Depression, he went further. he
created another trust—The Earhart foundation. Mother
and we four children were the permanent Trustees with
him. Our respective spouses as they came along were
elected Members. The Foundation had three purposes, the
first of which was the legal one of course: to contribute
funds to charitable, religious, and educational causes. The
next was to give his family training in the wise
administration of such gifts. The third he stated this way:

> It is also hoped the functioning as Trustees will
> develop a common interest that will tend to
> bring the family group into personal contact at
> regular intervals and be a tie to bind them
> together as a family group in such common
> interests.

How well his hopes were realized forms a story by
itself—the story of the Earhart Foundation.